JUPITER

by Emma Bassier

Cody Koala
An Imprint of Pop!
popbooksonline.com

abdobooks.com

Published by Pop!, a division of ABDO, PO Box 398466, Minneapolis, Minnesota 55439. Copyright © 2021 by POP, LLC. International copyrights reserved in all countries. No part of this book may be reproduced in any form without written permission from the publisher. Pop!™ is a trademark and logo of POP, LLC.

Printed in the United States of America, North Mankato, Minnesota.

102020
012021

THIS BOOK CONTAINS RECYCLED MATERIALS

Cover Photos: iStockphoto, Jupiter, background
Interior Photos: iStockphoto, 1 (Jupiter), 1 (background), 5 (top), 5 (bottom right), 15 (top background); NASA, 5 (bottom left), 9, 10, 13, 15 (bottom left), 15 (bottom right); Shutterstock Images, 6–7, 15 (top foreground), 16, 19 (top), 19 (bottom left), 19 (bottom right); Science & Society Picture Library/SPPL/Getty Images, 20

Editor: Alyssa Krekelberg
Series Designer: Colleen McLaren

Library of Congress Control Number: 2020940297
Publisher's Cataloging-in-Publication Data
Names: Bassier, Emma, author.
Title: Jupiter / by Emma Bassier
Description: Minneapolis, Minnesota : POP!, 2021 | Series: Planets | Includes online resources and index
Identifiers: ISBN 9781532169083 (lib. bdg.) | ISBN 9781532169441 (ebook)
Subjects: LCSH: Jupiter (Planet)--Juvenile literature. | Planets--Juvenile literature. | Solar system--Juvenile literature. | Milky Way--Juvenile literature. | Space--Juvenile literature.
Classification: DDC 523.45--dc23

Hello! My name is

Cody Koala

Pop open this book and you'll find QR codes like this one, loaded with information, so you can learn even more!

Scan this code* and others like it while you read, or visit the website below to make this book pop.

popbooksonline.com/jupiter

*Scanning QR codes requires a web-enabled smart device with a QR code reader app and a camera.

Table of Contents

Chapter 1
The Largest Planet 4

Chapter 2
Gas Giant. 8

Chapter 3
Spinning Fast 14

Chapter 4
Many Moons 18

Making Connections 22
Glossary. 23
Index 24
Online Resources 24

Chapter 1

The Largest Planet

Jupiter is the biggest planet in our **solar system**. It is so large that more than 1,300 Earths could fit in it.

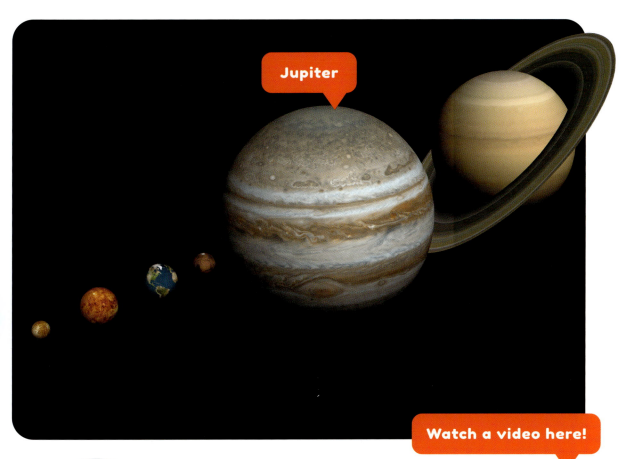

Jupiter

Watch a video here!

5

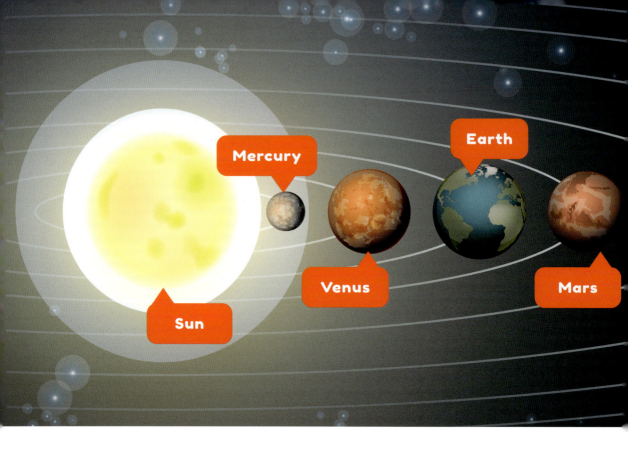

Our solar system has eight planets. The planets **orbit** the Sun. Jupiter is the fifth planet.

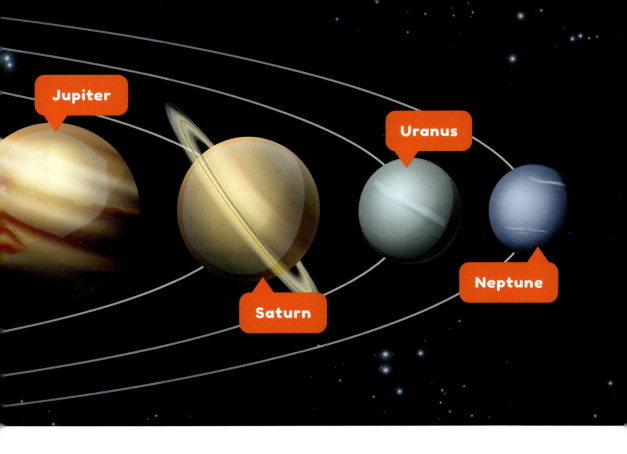

It is far away from the Sun. Jupiter only gets a little heat from the Sun. It is very cold.

The temperature in Jupiter's clouds can reach −229 degrees Fahrenheit (−145°C).

Chapter 2

Gas Giant

Jupiter is huge and made of gas. So, scientists call it a gas giant. Unlike Earth, a gas giant does not have a hard surface to stand on.

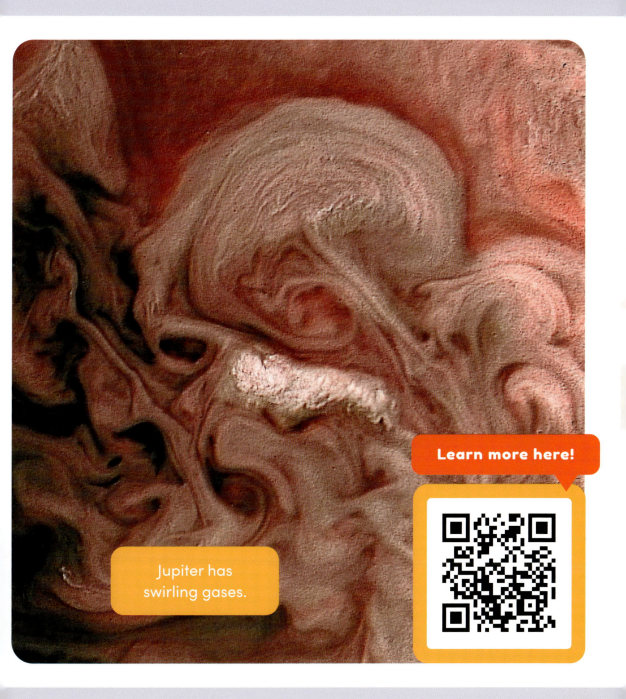

Jupiter has swirling gases.

Learn more here!

Jupiter has stripes and spots of color. Some of its colors are white, brown, red, and orange. Jupiter's colors come from the gases in the planet's **atmosphere**.

Jupiter is named after the king of the Roman gods.

The outside of Jupiter is windy. Storms blow across the planet. One storm can be seen from space. It is called the Great Red Spot. The storm has lasted hundreds of years.

Chapter 3

Spinning Fast

Each planet spins on its **axis**. One full spin is the length of a day. Jupiter has the shortest day of all the planets. Its day is only ten hours long.

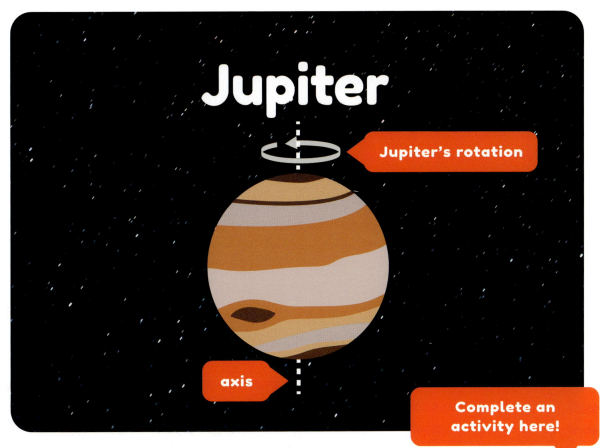

Jupiter

Jupiter's rotation

axis

Complete an activity here!

One lap around the Sun is the length of one year. Jupiter takes a long time to **orbit** the Sun. Its year is nearly 12 Earth years long.

Chapter 4

Many Moons

Jupiter has more than 50 moons. Scientists are still discovering them. Each moon **orbits** the planet. Most of the moons are made of rock and ice.

Jupiter's Largest Moons

Callisto

Europa

Ganymede

Io

Learn more here!

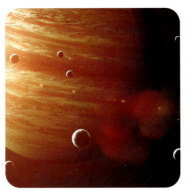

A large rocket launched the spacecraft going to Jupiter.

Jupiter has faint rings. The rings are made of dust. They are not easy to see. Scientists first saw Jupiter's rings in 1979. A **spacecraft** took pictures of them. People are still learning a lot about Jupiter.

Making Connections

Text-to-Self

If you were a scientist, which planet would you want to send a spacecraft to? Why would you choose that one?

Text-to-Text

Have you read other books about planets? How are those planets similar to or different from Jupiter?

Text-to-World

Jupiter's Great Red Spot is a giant storm. Can you think of some kinds of storms that happen on Earth?

Glossary

atmosphere – the layers of gases that surround a planet.

axis – an imaginary line that runs through the middle of a planet, from top to bottom.

orbit – to follow a rounded path around another object.

solar system – a collection of planets and other space material orbiting a star.

spacecraft – a vehicle that is used to explore space.

Index

atmosphere, 11

axis, 14, 15

gas, 8, 11

Great Red Spot, 12

moons, 18

rings, 21

solar system, 4, 6

Sun, 6, 7, 17

Online Resources

popbooksonline.com

Thanks for reading this Cody Koala book!

Scan this code* and others like it in this book, or visit the website below to make this book pop!

popbooksonline.com/jupiter

*Scanning QR codes requires a web-enabled smart device with a QR code reader app and a camera.